Managing Change

The Lessons Learned Series

Through the power of personal storytelling, each book in the Lessons Learned series presents the accumulated wisdom of some of the world's best known experts, and offers insights into how these individuals think, how they approach new challenges, and how they use hard-won lessons from experience to shape their leadership philosophies. Organized thematically, according to the topics at the top of managers' agendas, each book draws from Fifty Lessons' extensive video library of interviews with CEOs and other thought leaders. Here, the world's leading senior executives, academics, and business thinkers speak directly and candidly about their triumphs and defeats. Taken together, these powerful stories offer the advice you'll need to take on tomorrow's challenges.

Other books in the series:

Leading by Example
Managing Your Career

LESSONS LEARNED

Managing Change

Harvard Business School Press
Boston, Massachusetts

Copyright 2007 Fifty Lessons Limited
All rights reserved

Printed in the United States of America
11 10 09 08 07   5 4 3 2 1

No part of this publication may be reproduced, stored in or introduced into a retrieval system, or transmitted, in any form, or by any means (electronic, mechanical, photocopying, recording, or otherwise), without the prior permission of the publisher. Requests for permission should be directed to permissions@hbsp.harvard.edu, or mailed to Permissions, Harvard Business School Publishing, 60 Harvard Way, Boston, Massachusetts 02163.

Library of Congress Cataloging-in-Publication Data
Managing change.
    p. cm. — (Lessons learned)
  ISBN-13: 978-1-4221-1858-0 (pbk. : alk. paper)
 1. Organizational change. 2. Organizational effectiveness.
3. Management. 4. Communication in organizations.
I. Harvard Business School Publishing Corporation.
  HD58.8.M2543 2007
  658.4'06—dc22

                              2007019476

⇥ A NOTE FROM THE ⇤
PUBLISHER

In partnership with Fifty Lessons, a leading provider of digital media content, Harvard Business School Press is pleased to announce the launch of Lessons Learned, a new book series that showcases the trusted voices of the world's most experienced leaders. Through the power of personal storytelling, each book in this series presents the accumulated wisdom of some of the world's best-known experts and offers insights into how these individuals think, approach new challenges, and use hard-won lessons from experience to shape their leadership philosophies. Organized thematically according to the topics at the top of managers' agendas—leadership, change management, entrepreneurship, innovation, and strategy, to name a few—each book draws from Fifty Lessons' extensive video library of interviews with CEOs and other thought leaders.

A Note from the Publisher

Here, the world's leading senior executives, academics, and business thinkers speak directly and candidly about their triumphs and defeats. Taken together, these powerful stories offer the advice you'll need to take on tomorrow's challenges.

We invite you to join the conversation now. You'll find both new ways of looking at the world, and the tried-and-true advice you need to illuminate the path forward.

CONTENTS

1. Peter Birch
   Don't Delay Change   1

2. John Whybrow
   Change Today, Not Tomorrow   7

3. Laura Tyson
   Don't Let Bureaucracy Block Change   13

4. David Brandon
   Change Is Good   21

5. Sir Nick Scheele
   Change Comes Through Consistent Communication   29

6. William Harrison
   You Must Adapt to Change   37

7. James Strachan
   Change Is Simple   43

Contents

8. Shelly Lazarus
   Make It Comfortable to Take a Risk — 47

9. John Roberts
   Dealing with Opposition to Culture Change — 53

10. Maurice Lévy
    Reinventing an Organization — 57

11. Stephen Tindale
    Repositioning an Organization — 61

12. Mel Lagomasino
    Know When to Fold Your Hand — 67

13. Paul Skinner
    Monitor Your Business Environment and Anticipate Change — 73

14. John Abele
    Changing a Culture to Create a New Market — 79

About the Contributors — 87
Acknowledgments — 97

Managing Change

LESSON ONE

Don't Delay Change

Peter Birch

Former Chairman, Land Securities Group

I WAS APPOINTED a nonexecutive director of Argos, the catalog retailer. It was the first nonexecutive position I had, and I welcomed it because Argos has a number of retail networks—several hundred in fact—and had been highly successful. I was the only nonexecutive director to begin with; we recruited another one.

Managing Change

The executives had been there all their working lives; there'd been no changes whatsoever; and the chief executive, Dr. Mike Smith, had been hugely successful. He was revered in the City and couldn't put a foot wrong. All seemed to go well at Argos until he began to slow down; he was a heavy smoker, and nobody realized at the time that he was ill. He tried to keep going. Unfortunately, he had cancer. The cancer took hold of him, and he was unable to make decisions; this went on for a couple of years. No decisions were made, we weren't progressing as we had done, and he was very much the boss in control. It transpired that his management team, who had all worked for him since the day he'd started, were yesmen, and therefore there was no real debate in the board and no desire to change.

As a nonexecutive director, I tried to force change dramatically. I was rude at board meetings; I made a scene. I tried the other approach of being level-headed to try to get change through, but he was not up to it. He began to miss board meetings—he

Managing Change

didn't want to admit that he had cancer although we knew secretly that he did—and eventually he had to take time off work. At about the same time, the financial director became ill, but he and the chief executive were still pulling the strings behind the scenes. The City was still supportive of them, and the chairman was too, but one could see that the business was not going that well.

At our weakest moment, Great Universal Stores (GUS) made an offer for the business. At about the same time the chief executive died, the financial director went on ill-health retirement. I was appointed interim chairman. I recruited Stuart Rose—who eventually emerged at Arcadia, the big food group, as a chief executive—to fight the bid from GUS. We appointed Schroders as our advisers, and we worked very, very hard for the three months that it takes for these things to unfold. On the last day we had 45 percent of the votes, GUS had 45 percent, and Schroders had 10 percent. We thought that with Schroders acting for us they would

Managing Change

give us the votes, but their asset management side, which owned the 10 percent, decided they needed the cash, and they sided with GUS. So we lost the battle.

So what does one learn from that? One learns that when one sees signs of change in a team and the leader's eye going off the ball for whatever reason—illness or whatever—one needs to effect change and be ready to make change. That was certainly the case at Argos. It's a very sad case because what Dr. Mike Smith had done as chief executive—his ideas and the planning that he put in place—were all brilliant. All of those ideas, which were all in their embryo stage, were picked up by GUS and implemented. When they made the acquisition some four or five years ago, it was said that they paid a high price for Argos; in fact we got them to pay more than they originally expected to pay, but since then they've just gone from strength to strength.

They've done outstandingly well, implementing what we, as a board, knew needed to be done when we were an inde-

Managing Change

pendent organization. If it needs to be done and it's in the interests of the business, then one needs to effect change no matter how nasty it is and how much it impacts people. Very often it's kind to be hard—much kinder to be harder with people so that they understand it and know where they stand, rather than to be soft and let a bad situation get worse.

TAKEAWAYS

- If change needs to happen in the interests of the business, you must act—no matter how nasty it may seem or how much it impacts on staff or colleagues.

- It's often much kinder to be hard with people so they know where they stand, rather than be soft and let a bad situa-

Managing Change

tion get worse. You should encourage open communication between departments and be aware of problems and risks as soon as possible.

- You should always have contingency plans in place so you can quickly and effectively respond to problems by changing direction.

LESSON TWO

Change Today, Not Tomorrow

John Whybrow

Chairman, Wolseley

MANAGERS LOVE TO TALK about managing change. They love to implement change on others, but not so much on themselves, of course. They're always immune to it and think, "It's other people who should change—I'm OK!"

What drives this issue of change? Well, it's a changing world. Things change outside,

Managing Change

not inside; the environment starts to change. As that environment changes, we, as managers and directors, need to change our business to meet our objectives.

It may be that a nation becomes very powerful in an industry sector, like the Japanese did with electronics. Companies like Sony, Panasonic, Matsushita, and Pioneer are very fine electronics companies that became very successful. They basically put most of the American electronics consumer enterprises out of business; they either went bankrupt or were sold and bought by Japanese or European companies.

When I was at Philips, it was one of those companies under attack—our results became progressively more difficult (that's a management phrase that means "getting bad"). By the late 1980s, they were pretty bad; by the early 1990s they were awful; then there was an incident where a profit warning was not given when it should have been, and the president lost his job.

Suddenly Philips realized it had to do something; it couldn't ignore what was

Managing Change

going on in the world. It had always thought, "The exchange rates will change," or it had thought, "We're Philips, we're big. We're the biggest in Europe and one of the top three in the world. We're safe, we can handle this sort of thing." We couldn't. If only we'd looked at those issues five or ten years earlier, we wouldn't have had a dramatic issue on our plate.

Two hundred managers from across the world all got together in a conference room in Holland and decided that we had to be very dramatic. We took out 30 percent of our population across the world. Just to put that into numbers, that's about eighty thousand to ninety thousand people. When you apply that draconian approach locally, managers say, "You can't do that; you can't take out that many. The business will die. We can't survive."

The funny thing was, no businesses died. Every business survived, and even became better and stronger for it. We improved productivity hugely in circumstances where people said, "If we take out this number of

Managing Change

people, we won't be able to do our job properly." The top-level managers resisted that change because they were too late in taking the action. In the middle, people resisted it because they felt it was too dramatic and severe on the business. Then, when we actually forced it to happen, people were amazed at how well the business worked, having made those major changes.

Philips was one of two large electronics companies in Europe that survived, the other one being Siemens. And it's still a tough business. But they're both still there, to their credit. But if only we'd made those changes earlier, there wouldn't have had to be so much blood spilled to get to a good business situation.

As managers and directors, we are slow to respond. There is a cognitive dissonance in us whereby we convince ourselves that it's not really that bad, or it will recover—we don't have to do anything now, we can wait for tomorrow. We shouldn't wait for tomorrow. We should act now.

Managing Change

My message in the management of change is: if you see something happening out there, don't assume it will come back to where you want it to be. The world is not going to be in our model, the world will do what it wants to do. We must respond today, not tomorrow.

TAKEAWAYS

- You should always keep abreast of what's going on in the wider world. If you can the warning signs of imminent change, you can be nimble about responding to them.

- Complacency and lack of action is often bad for business. However, change is painful, and many people

Managing Change

will resist it. You must be prepared to push initiatives through if necessary.

- You must consistently monitor your results, discuss them at board level, and use them as a spur for action sooner rather than later.

LESSON THREE

Don't Let Bureaucracy Block Change

Laura Tyson

Former White House National Economic Adviser

ONE OF THE THINGS we talk to business students a lot about is the resistance of organizations to change. And a lot of what we try to study is what makes organizations

Managing Change

more or less flexible. Even if organizations are committed to flexibility, modes of behavior get entrenched in habits and rules. So the question is, if you're brought into an organization, particularly a relatively large organization, and you know that it is very rule ridden and bureaucracy ridden, how can you effectuate an important change that you believe really essential to the longevity of that institution?

This happened to me when I was approached to be the Dean of the [Haas School of Business] at the University of California at Berkeley. I knew enough about the institution to know that it was bureaucracy ridden, because I had been in and out of that institution as a professor for many years. I also knew that the organization absolutely needed a couple of new programs, for both revenue reasons, just simply to generate revenue income to support expansion, and reputational reasons, to reach out more effectively to the business community and build the reputation of the school.

Managing Change

So I knew new programs were essential. I also knew that one new program had been under consideration in that organization for nine years—nine years. I had not been there during this period; I'd been in Washington and doing other things. As I was being approached to take this organization on, one of the things I became absolutely certain about was that I needed to negotiate in the contract, for me, the possibility of breaking down some of these barriers.

One of these lessons is that, if you are asked to lead an organization, while you're negotiating the terms of your own personal contract, you should very much understand the things you should negotiate to allow you to lead that organization. And if it means breaking down some traditional rules, you should get that in the contract. So I did do that.

Now how did I do that? This gets to the second point about how one might get around bureaucracy—the idea of an experimental process. If the rules are very rigid,

Managing Change

what you might do is say, "Let's try something on an experimental basis. It can be relatively small. Let's say we do it for three years, and we set a review process in motion. Everyone knows at the end of three years we will look at it." If you truly believe in the change you're making, then you're taking a bet that the experiment will be a big success, everybody will applaud it, and it will become essentially a permanent entity.

So I did that. I argued that we're going to have to go around the rules. But I will respect the rules for now while I try this experiment out, if you will give me experimental flexibility. So a second point is, if you can't change the rules from the beginning—I did a little of that in some cases—just do an experiment. The experiment, by the way, led to programs that exist to this day, which are a major source of revenue for that institution that I led.

A third thing is just persistence. I'm sure that we probably don't use that word enough in business education, but we do use the

Managing Change

word *focus* a lot. And I think focus and persistence are different ways of saying the same thing. Leaders have to decide what their priorities are; if one says that, that's correct. They have to focus on their priorities and not get deflected; they have to persist in the belief that those priorities are the right ones in order, ultimately, to get anything done.

So when I said I negotiated a contract, I got the right to develop some experiments. But actually it wasn't like, "And, therefore, we developed these programs." There were many, many steps, and that was the persistence part—going to meetings, and when you hit a barrier, making a call to the president of the university and saying, "Look, this is what my contract says; this is the experiment; someone is blocking me. I need to get past that."

So persistence, persistence, persistence. And if you're right, if you set the right goal to achieve, the right program to put in place, persistence, I think, will result in success.

Managing Change

TAKEAWAYS

- Even organizations committed to flexibility have modes of behavior entrenched in habits and rules. If you're considering a position of leadership in such an organization, you would be wise to negotiate into your contract the things that will allow you to lead necessary changes.

- To circumvent bureaucracy, you should suggest changes on an experimental basis, making sure to define a trial period. These experiments may later become permanent.

Managing Change

⚔ To accomplish your goals, you must remain focused, avoid distraction, and trust that your priorities are the right ones. The process may not be easy, but you must remain steadfast.

LESSON FOUR

Change Is Good

David Brandon

Chairman and CEO, Domino's Pizza

EARLY IN MY LIFE I was a student athlete at the University of Michigan, and it was a wonderful opportunity for me to get my first lessons in the world of management because I had great coaches. I played on a football team that won thirty games, lost one, and tied one in three years. We won the championship all three years, so it was a very high level of performance, great coaches,

Managing Change

and a lot of really good players. I didn't play a lot in those days. I was on the team, and I was proud to be so, but I got a chance to observe a lot—sometimes more than I wanted to—from the perspective of how the coaches prepared the team to win.

One of the things that fascinated me was that, in the game of football, there is a situation that's probably one of the hardest to deal with—what we call *sudden change*. What it meant was that the defense would come off the field and they'd be tired; they'd be looking for water and they'd want to sit down and rest. They wouldn't even get to the spot on the bench where they'd be comfortable before the offense would fumble the ball or throw an interception, or have some situation occur that would be the most negative thing for a defense you could imagine, because it meant they had to go right back out there without any rest and usually defend in a situation that was very, very negative.

What I found fascinating was that the coaches were actually able to forecast that this

Managing Change

was going to happen throughout the season, and they prepared the team for it. At practice we actually used to go through mock drills of sudden change. What they taught us to do whenever that nasty situation occurred was to all shout, "Sudden change!" and we would all get together as a team, grab hands, and seize this as an opportunity. In other words, we were programmed to believe that when this very negative situation occurred, rather than responding negatively we would actually see it as an opportunity, get excited about it, and anticipate it in a way that we knew we were going to be successful.

I later in life determined that that was a great lesson that could be applied to the world of business. Because if organizations understand that change is good, and when you are confronted with change—particularly change that is challenging—a great organization is going to be ready for that, they're going to anticipate it and see it as an opportunity. I really adopted my own version of sudden change in business,

Managing Change

and my phrase is called "Change is good." Throughout my organization, whenever we encounter something that was not anticipated, particularly something that has some negative connotations to it, we'll look at one another and we'll say, "Change is good. This is an opportunity for us to react to change, make it positive, and apply ourselves in a way that allows us to step up and accomplish something important."

We tend to resist change because often change creates problems that require solutions, and sometimes those solutions require a lot of extra work. So if you understand that people are going to approach change with trepidation, and some are going to resist it, I think as a leader the way that you can best prepare your organization is to transform their thinking and put them in a mind-set that makes them want to embrace change.

When I was introduced on my first day as the CEO of Domino's Pizza, I was kind of wheeled out from behind a blue curtain. I

Managing Change

was not someone who had been here as part of the team. It was a thirty-eight-year-old company, and I was the second CEO, the first one to follow the founder and pioneer who created the business. So I come from behind the curtain, and there's hundreds of people politely applauding but mostly wanting to know what this new guy is all about and what we are in for under this new generation of leadership.

I decided that my remarks would be very, very brief but hopefully would set the tone. What I said to the group was, "If you are the kind of people and the type of organization that loves change, that believes that change is good, change is exciting, and embracing change is something that you really want to get good at and want to do, then you're going to love me. If you're the kind of person who wants things always to be the way they've been and you want to sit around and talk about the good old days, then I'm not your guy, because truthfully I'm here to create better days, and that's going to require change."

Managing Change

TAKEAWAYS

⚜ People are scared of change because it represents a break from their working habits and a lot of extra work. You should reinforce that change is good and create an association with opportunity and excitement that will encourage people to embrace rather than fear it.

⚜ You must be firm and set the tone from the start: change is good and is a part of your leadership strategy. Chance can be a route to success. You must make it clear that anyone who doesn't like change will either need to embrace the idea or reconsider his or her options.

Managing Change

⚜ During a period of change, you should concentrate on internal PR, and continue to communicate the positive opportunities associated with the project.

LESSON FIVE

Change Comes Through Consistent Communication

Sir Nick Scheele

*Former President and
Chief Operating Officer,
Ford Motor Company*

Managing Change

WHEN I WENT TO JAGUAR in 1992, a predecessor of mine, John Egan, had started regular dialogues with the entire workforce and had done so for a long time. John then moved on to BAA. I arrived and I thought this regular dialogue was a great thing to do. So I carried on with it, and twice a year I used to spend a week—sometimes about eight or nine days in fact—communicating with the entire workforce through four or five sessions every day.

It was a lot of work because I would do it all. It would be a communication session of about an hour and a half and then a gap of half an hour as people shuttled in. You might say, "Well, why didn't you do it once and get everybody there?" and the answer was that we didn't have a theater, hall, or room big enough to take everybody—and we certainly couldn't afford the money to hire a theater outside to which we could have bused everybody, because that would have been money that we needed for other things.

So I communicated. I would take people through exactly where the company stood

Managing Change

in terms of the profit forecast, sales, quality, and orders that were coming in and what that might or might not do to the outlooks for full work—because at this time we were only working about three days a week, and some weeks we had no days to work because we just didn't have the orders. I did this, in fact, throughout the seven years that I was at Jaguar.

I did it twice a year for those seven years, and I think it was good that I started off my first month at Jaguar doing this because it was a very difficult period. It was Jaguar's lowest year in terms of sales. We were going to have to make layoffs; we were going to have to take some very difficult decisions.

The reasons for those decisions were not immediately obvious, but they had to be put in context of the overall plan and where we wanted to get to, moving forward. We also talked about that with the workforce twice a year, and we would take any questions from them as well, so that they could ask, "Why is it that we're not selling more?" Or, "Why is it that we want to make this particular car

Managing Change

rather than that particular car?" Or, "Why this engine, and why do it there rather than elsewhere?"

And we had to give them the information. We had to do it in a consistent fashion. It was no good one time in January, say, to use these sets of data and then in July to come back with a totally different set of data. We had to be consistent if we wanted to improve our quality. We used JD Power results as the driver for quality—as the metric, if you will—of where we stood on quality.

We used sales penetration, we used profit line, we used productivity, and we used consistent measures. Communicating and being consistent over time in how you communicate builds up trust because people see the same graphs, the same bar charts, the same sets of data. They see them time after time, and they see that you're not trying to play games with them, because if it changes people say, "Why did they change? Was there a hidden agenda there?"

Managing Change

So communicating was very important. It turned out to be hugely important because it was, I think, one of the key platforms that the whole workforce could get behind: they knew they were part of solving the bigger problem, which was how to get Jaguar back to where it deserved to be. And they felt, as I still believe to this day, that they were part of the solution—and a major part of the solution—because they knew all the facts. And as they knew all the facts, they became much more involved, much more proactive, and much more desirous of seeing a different result coming into the bottom line and, of course, in sales.

They were fascinating sessions. I used to enjoy them, although they were very tiring because there was the night shift as well to do, so it wasn't just a question of doing it from 9 a.m. to 5 p.m. And they were rewarding. They were rewarding because you could see change and you could see it starting to happen and, most importantly, you could see people's confidence starting to

Managing Change

build. They could fix it; they would fix it. We have fixed it. And it happened.

I learned several things from those many, many sessions. One: be totally honest; don't ever try to prevaricate, because if you do you'll answer somebody in one way and you won't quite give them the truth. You'll shave the truth or not give them the whole story, and then sometime in the future somebody will ask you a very similar question and you won't remember what you said in the other session. And then, of course, your credibility is shot and all the good that you've done is just totally destroyed. So be totally honest.

Two: be consistent. Don't come up with new sets of data; be very consistent in how you show things.

And three: when you communicate, don't look as though you hate it; enjoy it, because you are working with people—and if they don't trust you, if they believe that you think this is a waste of your time, they won't follow you. They will only follow you if they believe in you and they see that you believe in them.

Managing Change

TAKEAWAYS

- Using a consistent set of key performance indicators combined with regular communication will help you to build trust between you and your team.

- Regular communication with your team can provide a key platform for generating support among your people by making them feel part of the solution; a workforce that knows all the facts will become much more involved, proactive, and desirous of seeing a different result in the bottom line.

- Your team will not follow you if they don't trust you or if you appear to think that communicating is a waste of time; they will follow you only if they believe in you and can see that you believe in them.

LESSON SIX

You Must Adapt to Change

William Harrison

*Former Chairman and CEO,
JPMorgan Chase & Co.*

I THINK THE ABILITY to change is so important. Everybody talks about it all the time, and when I lead a leadership class and start talking about this, you can almost see people's eyes roll—you know, *"Of course* we have to change." But the fact of the matter is, change is hard. People fundamentally

Managing Change

don't like it. Some people are better at it than others. And so my message is, we are in a changing world. It is not going to stop, and the more you can adapt to change and be a leader of change, the better off you're going to be.

How does that play out? Well, it plays out in a very simple form. You as a leader, go in. You have ten people on a team, and you say, "Okay, here's the challenge, and it's tough." And, very quickly, you'll see some people who will say, "Oh my gosh, why do we have to do that again? This is hard. Do we really have to do this? I'm tired of doing it." Or something similar.

Well, that's not good because that person begins to suck the energy out of everybody. So, compare that person to the person who says, "Yes. That's a really tough project, but we're going to all jump on it, give it our best, and let's go figure it out. Whatever it is, let's go figure it out."

Now, who do you want on your team? If you're building a team, what kind of person do you want on your team? I think it's very

Managing Change

clear. You want people with this positive, can-do attitude who are willing to look at change as an opportunity instead of a problem or a threat. And again, while that's a very simple example, it does play out that way, and so what you want to do is weed out those people who can't jump on the boat and paddle it forward, because they will slow you down.

When I talk about the ability to change, I think of a couple of interesting examples that go beyond just individuals. I've talked about the importance of individuals being willing or able to change, but let's talk about two examples of a country or a company.

Now let's take Japan. In the mid-1980s, Japan was being viewed by most knowledgeable people as the new economic superpower in the world. The United States was losing altitude; we were not competing well. Japan was the winner, it looked like. By the end of the 1980s, Japan began to hit a wall, and one of the reasons they began to hit a wall is that globalization—the speed of globalization—which is all about change, picked

Managing Change

up. And I would argue that their system was unable to change as quickly as it needed to. Here it is, twelve or thirteen years later, and they are just beginning to get some growth back into that economy.

But that is a good example of a culture; it was a great culture: Japan, Inc. They did a lot of wonderful things, great people. But that culture, how the political system worked, and how they ran companies in many situations prevented them from changing fast enough in a really accelerating global environment.

Another example would be IBM. IBM in the 1970s, the early 1980s, was perhaps the greatest company in the country—maybe in the world—in terms of reputation, image, and how they were run. They had a very strong culture. This same culture that made them a great company actually got in the way of their ability to change. They didn't think they needed to change; it was part of their mind-set: "We are really good." So their business changed. They weren't able to

Managing Change

change quickly enough. They almost failed. Lou Gerstner came in and finally was able to take advantage of the strengths of the company and change.

So we see this whole notion of change, the ability to change, being played out all the time in countries, in companies, and in individuals.

TAKEAWAYS

- ⚜ The more individuals and organizations are equipped and able to adapt to change, the more likely their chance of success. You, as an individual, must also be prepared for change.

- ⚜ It's important for you to identify team members who see change as a positive force and remove those who perceive

Managing Change

change in a negative light. You can use the positive energy to bring the doubters along.

- You must be on guard for signs of slow-down. The inability to move quickly and the complacency that results from arrogance are just two of the inhibitors to successfully weathering change.

LESSON SEVEN

Change Is Simple

James Strachan

*Former Chairman,
Audit Commission, UK*

THIS IS A LESSON I learned about how to manage change. I was advising a major U.K. conglomerate, and I remember being very struck by the chief executive telling me with absolute dogmatism that change is preciously simple—which actually isn't what most people tell you.

Managing Change

He said, "All you have to do is to figure out precisely where you want to go, and you need to be able to paint that 'promised land' in Technicolor.

Second, you need to ask whether you've got the right people around you, particularly at the top; if not, change them tomorrow—literally tomorrow.

Third, you delegate; but you do so without actually absolving yourself of all responsibility. You still own the ultimate responsibility—the buck stops with you—but you significantly delegate to people to enable them to bring out the best in themselves.

Last, you praise their success to high heaven."

It may sound very simplistic to some people, but actually in times of really stressful change where you're trying to get people to go over the barricades and go against their natural desire to keep things pretty much as they are, this kind of simple, forceful, confident, full-of-conviction leadership is gold dust.

Managing Change

When people look at dominant leadership, it's interesting how they get very concerned about "top-down" command and control, which is a very pejorative concept to most people.

It's perfectly possible to have inspiring leadership at the top but through good management actually cascade messages all the way through the organization about where we want to go and how we can get there. Good management inspires people at all levels in the organization, not just the general at the top who makes a rousing Prince Hal speech from time to time.

The lesson about change for me is that in times of change there's a lot of turbulence, confusion, worry, and concern. This is all natural. So people naturally gravitate toward a leadership that tries to take this confusion and describe it in simple terms about why we are doing this, what the "promised land" that we're going to get to is, and why all this agony is worthwhile. In times of change, it is simplicity and conviction that rule.

Managing Change

TAKEAWAYS

- There are four steps to simple change: a clear purpose of direction that is effectively communicated; assurance that the right people are in place; delegation to ensure those people are properly involved; and continuous praise of successes.

- If a project within your organization requires changing, you must not shirk from that process. You will need to work out a time line and plan for action, and communicate your intentions properly to everyone involved.

- You should be prepared to establish regular updates on action—either written reports or a meeting—to make sure everyone is fully involved.

LESSON EIGHT

Make It Comfortable to Take a Risk

Shelly Lazarus

*Chairman and CEO,
Ogilvy & Mather Worldwide*

SO MUCH OF WHAT WE DO for clients is new, innovative, breakthrough. And when you're in this area of high creativity and innovation, you're always dealing with risk,

Managing Change

because you're trying things that have never been tried before. So much of what my job is in leading the agency is to make it comfortable to take a risk, to champion ideas when they're very young and fragile, and, because they are so young and fragile, to figure out how to get people to believe in them enough that they can live. And this seems sort of easy and trite, but it's probably the hardest thing we do.

Here's how it happens: someone has a crazy idea, and they kind of throw it out there to see how people react. And you can't be too judgmental at the start, because you need to give them a little support and let them breathe a little bit. Let them live and see where the idea goes.

The IBM campaign was one of the great creative journeys of my life. It started with a twenty-six-year-old writer who had only been in the business for about two years and who was out in our Los Angeles office. He had this really zany idea to do commercials in many different languages—not usual

Managing Change

ones; he started with one in Czech—and to run subtitles on the bottom, as a way of saying that technology is universal and that the solutions that technology is coming up with actually bring our world together and are present everywhere. It started with a script that described nuns in a cloister who would be coming towards you, speaking Czech. They would be talking about the new software program that was about to be introduced by IBM. And there were some funny little bits of business, like one of the nun's beepers was going off.

So, you had all these issues. First of all, you were dealing with the church, the clergy. You were going to a client in Westchester with a script that was in Czech with subtitles. And you had to be pretty brave—you had to believe that this was an idea that could go further. And so we did take it further. We went to cowboys in Argentina, riding on the Pampas, talking about PCs. And two old Frenchmen walking by the Seine, talking about servers. So, before we actually went up

Managing Change

to see the client, we had to develop a degree of conviction that this was a big idea and an important idea and a large idea that could go everywhere in the world and would really put IBM, which was suffering at the time—it was not a strong brand at the time—in a new place in the world.

We went up, and we did the first presentation. And I kept sort of rolling my eyes, thinking, "I don't know how this is going. I don't know where this is going to come out." At the end, there was just sort of quiet. The clients asked a lot of questions. It was Abby Kohnstamm and Lou Gerstner, just the two of them. And in the end, they said, "This is brilliant. This is fantastic. We love it, and we're going to go with it," which was even braver, I thought, than the act of bringing it to them in the first place. And, as they say, the rest is history.

But it was so easy for that idea to die, at so many places, up to the point that it go to approval, that you had to be believers. You had to really support the idea, champion the idea, to get it to a point where it could live.

Managing Change

To me, it's not just in advertising; it's in everything. In all business, half the ideas aren't going to work—fewer than half the ideas will work, actually. So, if you have to have two great ideas, to me you have to have ten experiments going at all times, because only two of them are going to work. And to me, that's the fun. You're allowed to experiment; you're allowed to try things and to be wrong sometimes. And you have to institutionalize that part. You have to make it okay to be wrong.

TAKEAWAYS

- If you're a creative worker or the leader of one, you must learn how to make risk more comfortable.

- You need to let ideas breathe and give them a chance to grow, instead of being

Managing Change

judgmental and squashing creativity. Creativity can be a fragile commodity.

- ⚏ Because fewer than half of all ideas will come to fruition, it's critical for you to convey to staff and colleagues that it is okay to make mistakes. You must be prepared to champion their ideas.

LESSON NINE

Dealing with Opposition to Culture Change

John Roberts

*Former Chief Executive Officer,
United Utilities*

Managing Change

NOT EVERYBODY immediately sees the benefit of culture change stimulating performance, because not everybody wants to change.

In my experience, the people who are most likely to resist are those in junior and middle management—who have some degree of seniority, status, and reward, and all of a sudden you want to change that. The people at the top of the organization can probably see the bigger picture and understand why. The guys in the middle are thinking to themselves, "What's in this for me? Why should I change? I've been successful within the existing system, and I don't want to trade that in to change to something else in which maybe I won't be as successful."

That is one of the big difficulties you have to break through; there is a kind of permafrost that sits in the organization. You have to address that by first explaining very clearly to everybody, particularly those people most likely to resist, why you're doing what you're doing, that it is not a threat, and how the change will benefit them.

Managing Change

Persuade them to come on the journey with you because it will improve; they don't have to be threatened by it. One has to say that, on average, in any organization, about 15 percent of the people will go with the management whatever they do. About 15 percent don't really like the management at all and will resist them whatever they do. You're really playing to the 70 percent in the middle.

You move them, plus the other 15 percent, and about 85 percent of people are on your side. You have to be realistic about the balance and the objectives. There will always be some people who, whatever you do, don't want to know and don't want to change. Ultimately, with the best will in the world, what you have to say to those people is, "Look, we're all going in this direction; if you don't want to come with us, fine—you'd better go somewhere else because this is the kind of organization we're going to be."

In my experience, that is a very, very small proportion but, when you've tried everything and people just will not come onside, then

Managing Change

you have to take decisive action. Otherwise that will start to detract from what you're doing with the majority. That will then be a drag on performance, which you don't want.

TAKEAWAYS

- If you intend to undertake culture change, you must be prepared to explain why it is necessary in your organization. You will need to persuade staff to see the benefits of change, and act decisively with those people who continue to resist change.

- When you explain your culture change initiative to staff, you should hold a Q&A session so that they can ask their own questions. This is always preferable to the rumor mill working overtime.

⇥ LESSON TEN ⇤

Reinventing an Organization

Maurice Lévy

*Chairman and CEO,
Publicis Groupe*

ONE OF THE PROBLEMS we have as an ad agency is the fact that not only must we always deliver the best possible service to a client, always use the best tools available, and create some of the best programs, but—as life is not easy—we also need to cope with some of the constraints of our business.

Managing Change

So when there is a recession, we have to make sure that we can cope with it; and when there is a pick-up, that we don't have a huge rise in our cost.

The best way to do that is constantly to reinvent ourselves. In 1992 there was a very serious recession in France. Most—and when I say most, it was all—of our competitors had laid off something like 20 percent of their people. It was huge: 20 or 25 percent. There were companies or agencies that laid off much more—three hundred people, which is huge for an ad agency, perhaps 40 percent of their staff.

And we thought, "These people are not responsible for this crisis; these people have created our wealth, and to lay them off just because there is a recession seems unfair to them." So we tried to create something.

We created what we called "the economic revolution." This was a caucus over one month, every evening, where all the people in the agency met to try to find solutions. Then we came up with an idea: a referen-

Managing Change

dum asking if everyone was ready to cut their salaries, starting with the CEO, in order to avoid the layoffs.

It worked. Not only did it work, but we'd thought it would be necessary to cut salaries for two years; after *one* year we were able to reestablish the original salaries. So you see that by being innovative in the way you manage the structure and change it, and manage your people, you can find the resource for more energy and more talent, and create a culture that is shared by the people. They feel good about the company, they feel good about the way we care, and obviously they work much more. And at the end of the day, we win.

So never stabilize an organization; never think that the organization is forever. Always create an instability in the organization and make sure that you can move the borders—from one department to another, or one organization to another—very quickly. Be fast in creating the opportunity for reinventing yourself.

Managing Change

TAKEAWAYS

- ⚜ Keeping an organization flexible in its management and structure is the best way to ensure long-term stability. You must be prepared to do your part.

- ⚜ You should marshal your creative resources when implementing change. Thinking creatively about problems can often lead to satisfying win/win results.

- ⚜ You must be prepared to deal with anything—from possible layoffs to a hostile takeover bid. Reinvention can be a difficult process.

LESSON ELEVEN

Repositioning an Organization

Stephen Tindale

*Executive Director,
Greenpeace UK*

THERE HAS BEEN a lively debate in Greenpeace all over the world about to what extent we move away from our traditional issues into new agendas and into solutions. Some people are concerned that we're going to lose our radical edge and that we're going

Managing Change

to lose our emphasis on confrontation—as we put it, creative confrontation—to create space for new debates to happen.

My response to that, and the response to the directors of other Greenpeace offices around the world, is that it's a false dichotomy: You don't need to make that choice. Of course, to move in solutions work, we need to put a lot more emphasis on the positive. But there are plenty of things we need to propose, and often we need to propose them in very classic Greenpeace ways—going out onto the high seas and stopping things happening, for example. It's a question of looking across the range of what we're doing and saying, "We're still going to be the Greenpeace that everyone knows, and some love, but we're going to be doing things as well that the Greenpeace in the 1970s wouldn't have done."

As soon as I took over at Greenpeace, I was keen to put more emphasis onto the solutions side of our work. In fact, one of the objectives I set publicly was that after my

Managing Change

tenure, I wanted people to know as many things that Greenpeace was in favor of as things they were against. I knew that was a tall order, but I didn't know quite how tall an order until I spent the day at the Lowestoft air show a couple of summers ago.

It was a very hot day, and we had a mobile display stand, talking about offshore wind farms and the capacity of East Anglia to produce a quarter of the United Kingdom's electricity from offshore wind farms and to create sixty thousand jobs in the same time. We thought this was a good message, and we thought it would enable us to say to people that you don't need a new generation of nuclear power stations in East Anglia, which they were being threatened with.

People saw the logo of Greenpeace, which is of course very well known, and a lot of people came up to us. A lot of people were pleased to talk to us, but most of them were very surprised that we were speaking out in favor of offshore wind, in favor of anything. That's what they said. They said, "We didn't

Managing Change

know you had all of this to you. We thought that you were just an antinuclear and antiwhaling group." The sense that I had then was that we really needed to do a lot more to put out a positive agenda, because that's what we believe in, but also because that's what people want to hear from us.

The crucial point is that we've got to redesign. And we are redesigning the way we communicate with our own supporters and with the media, so that we put a lot more emphasis on what we're in favor of—if you like, the lead message is that this is the solution, this is what we want people to do about things. The environmental message generally about the state of the world, about the threats to the world, has come a long way in the thirty years since Greenpeace was founded. People are much more aware about issues, particularly the issue of climate change, which, given the changed weather patterns plus repeated warnings from scientists, means that people have now got the message that there's an issue out there. And they now want to know, "Okay we've

Managing Change

got that. What do we do about it? Let's move on."

For Greenpeace that is a tremendous opportunity. And if we get it right, we can be seen to be the bridge between people getting alarmed and wanting to take action to make things better and the solutions being available. It's very energizing for us as an organization to be working on solutions. And over the next three or four years, the intention is that we lead much more with our solutions work than with our campaigning against things.

TAKEAWAYS

- Organizations sometimes have difficulty moving away from traditional issues and into new agendas and solutions. You should remember that

Managing Change

people fear it may not possible to maintain the foundation on which the organization was built.

- You can present a new agenda in the same manner as an older one, thereby retaining your organization's identity. When repositioning an organization, you must be sure to communicate fully to staff, supporters, clients, and, if necessary, the media.

- As an organization grows, so do its members and its customers. You must remember to listen to them. Creating new agendas and solutions can create remarkable opportunities.

LESSON TWELVE

Know When to Fold Your Hand

Mel Lagomasino

*CEO, Asset Management Advisors,
an affiliate of SunTrust Banks, Inc.*

THIS IS THE TOUGHEST LESSON, I think; after you devote yourself to a company and to a lifelong career, and you've been very successful—as I have been lucky

Managing Change

enough to be—to be able to say, "We've come to the point where you need to step down." This is the time when you have to know when to fold them. I had been with [JP Morgan Private Bank] for twenty-three years, and had had the privilege of getting to the point where I wanted to be, of being able to run the private bank, arguably for the most prestigious company in the world.

We were about to go into another merger, another integration of private banks. I had already done five or six, and they are very painful to do. And I started to realize that the culture of the company we were merging with this time was going to be significantly different from the culture that I had grown up in. It wasn't that the culture would be better or worse; it was that it would be different. It would be different around the way we dealt with clients and the way we dealt with employees.

And I realized that there comes a time where you have to step back and ask, "What is it that's really important to me, and what

Managing Change

is it that makes me happy about working in this job? With this change that is coming, is this really what I'm going to want to do for the next X number of years?" And I realized that, culturally, what we were going to do was so different that I was going to have to make a very tough decision. I decided to fold my cards. I decided, at the top of my game, to step down—arguably from the world's most prestigious private bank—and I never looked back.

For me, I think the big lesson here is that no matter how great the title is, how great the company is, how long you've been there, or how much you enjoyed the run, there are points in time—particularly cultural points in time—when you need to step back and reassess, and ask, "Is this what I want to do for the next X number of years, and do I have a cultural fit?" And understand that even though it might have this—the company might have the same name it had before—the culture might not be the same as it was before. It's time to step down and start anew.

Managing Change

I think at the end of the day, when your values and how you like to work are totally simpatico with the values and the culture of the organization you work in, you have a very high probability of success, because in a sense you're swimming in your own element. If, in fact you have a disconnect between the two—and again, it's not about better or worse, or good and bad; it's just about different—then you really have to step back and ask, "What does this really mean, and do I want to put a stop to it here? Is it the time to fold them and move on and reinvent yourself?" And that's what I did.

TAKEAWAYS

- One of the toughest challenges you will face during a career is knowing when to step down from a position. When

Managing Change

the company faces a culture shift, you must reassess where you are and ask whether or not you should look for a change.

- When peoples' values and how they like to work are a good fit, there is a high probability of success. When peoples' values and how they like to work don't match, that's the time to reassess and determine whether it's time to move on. You must ask yourself where you fit in that continuum.

- As an employee, you should make a list of three problems that can occur when a leader stays in a position too long. Keep a copy of this list and revisit it annually as a reminder to reassess your own fit within the business.

LESSON THIRTEEN

Monitor Your Business Environment and Anticipate Change

Paul Skinner

Chairman, Rio Tinto

Managing Change

IT'S IMPORTANT for any organization to maintain an appropriate level of external focus by continuously scanning the business environment, thinking about changes that might take place, and being ready to respond to them with well-developed plans that are properly executed.

I remember—and I go back quite a long way, to the mid-1980s—when I was responsible for managing the Shell business in New Zealand. At this time, the country was undergoing fundamental economic change and restructuring.

For many years, New Zealand had been a highly regulated economy protected by tariff, lots of internal rules, and regulations and subsidies where appropriate. The country was building up significant levels of foreign debt, and it had reached a point where all this was becoming rather unsustainable.

The new government arrived and decided that they would embark upon a major program of economic deregulation and change. This led to the rapid dismantling of all these

Managing Change

controls and significantly changed the business environment for many industries in that country.

I was in the oil-refining and marketing business in New Zealand at the time, which, like many other industries, had been highly regulated. There were prescribed rates of return and margins on different phases of the business. As a major player, we were not allowed to own retail outlets, for example, so we were operating within a very tightly defined framework, which was really quite limiting.

As the deregulation flowed through the economy, all of that disappeared very quickly. We were allowed to own retail outlets, we could set our own prices, and we could invest where we wanted and reshape our retail network accordingly.

We had been thinking about this at Shell for a long time. We had been tracking the thoughts and opinions of the country's different political parties about our industry, and were constantly thinking on a scenario basis of how it might change.

Managing Change

As a result we'd had a contingency plan in place for some time to deal with the deregulation of our industry well in advance of these changes. As soon as the political winds started to change direction, we were able to activate that plan and significantly strengthen our position in the market. This came as a result of a very rapid rollout and execution of our deregulation plan, for which we had already agreed on an appropriate level of funding with our shareholders in Europe.

We were able to move much faster than most of our competitors as those changes came about. The major lesson from all this for me was that you'd better keep monitoring the business environment in which you operate, be ready to reinvent your business as the opportunities arrive, and be able to execute [your plan] well. I think we were able to do that: but it was really dependent upon continuous reappraisal of how our business environment might change.

Managing Change

TAKEAWAYS

- You must always try to be prepared for change, be ready to reinvent your business as the opportunities arrive, and to execute well. Even if change isn't on the direct horizon, you must always have a contingency plan.

- If your industry is dependent on international markets, you should monitor changing economic conditions and future growth markets. Whenever possible, you should try to glean intelligence from your competitors.

LESSON FOURTEEN

Changing a Culture to Create a New Market

John Abele

Cofounder, Boston Scientific

Managing Change

THIS LESSON IS SOMETHING that I didn't realize was a lesson until quite a while after it happened. We had developed a product called a steerable catheter, and one of the applications developed in the early 1970s for that was a technique for the nonoperative removal of gallstones. Another doctor in the United Kingdom, with whom our agent had been working, had developed a different technique: he'd used an endoscope to do the same thing. Ours was guided by X-ray; his was guided optically by fiber optics in the tube. We decided that it would be interesting to see how these two techniques compared, so the doctors came up with the idea: Why don't we have a competition?

This was in 1975, and we had this competition at the Middlesex Hospital in London. The contest was called a draw because the endoscopic technique was an elegant, fascinating tour de force, which the audience appreciated. But the radiologic technique was simple and could be applied by anyone,

Managing Change

because the learning skills were very easy. It was an important educational technique.

That experience, as it turns out, didn't influence the market right away, but over a number of years others were starting to copy that technique, and said, "Using this technique we can teach much more rapidly than we have done traditionally."

Not only that: "If this course is not sponsored by an establishment institution—the academic center or a professional society—then we don't have to worry about being politically correct and influencing people. We will have a course where there will be a live demonstration everybody can see, and there will be a panel of experts commenting continuously. In addition, everybody in the audience is equipped with a keypad." And sometimes these audiences would range up to ten thousand physicians, so it was a big, big deal.

Therefore, you in the audience would see a procedure being done. You could see not only the patient and the physician, but you

Managing Change

could also see inside them, because they would have X-rays or endoscopic pictures. You would see recent publications on the technique, clinical trials—both for and against, so you'd get a balanced representation of what a lot of people think—and then you'd hear experts arguing about it.

That enables you to have a real-time peer review. In addition to the peer review of experts, you also have the peer review of all your colleagues, who answer questions in parallel with the presentation. Questions are posted silently on a screen; you press a button to answer, like you do in some television programs, and the answer comes out. You can answer anonymously—nobody will know how you've voted, but you will know how all of your colleagues thought at the same time. Because this is continuous, and you are all learning, you will see how minds are being changed.

What makes this an interesting lesson—for me, anyway—was the fact that, at Boston Scientific, we were constantly introducing

Managing Change

very disruptive technology. By disruptive, I don't just mean new: disruptive means that you have to learn new skills; sometimes you are going to have to change the players, and if you do, you'll need new infrastructure. The economics are different, and the pathways in and out of the system are different. This is very threatening to the establishment, where the normal response would be, "Let's write about them," and "Show me your twenty-year results," which is exactly what they did. But this was an example where the physicians started voting with their feet. They said, "I want to go to this independent course because I learn more, and I think I trust this information more than the courses that are put on by my professional society."

For us, it collapsed the time frame for the development of these new technologies, because they don't spring perfectly formed into the marketplace; they go into the marketplace, and then they constantly evolve and iterate. This medical live demonstration

Managing Change

course enabled us to learn more as technologists—not just as companies. Not only did it enable us to understand the technical aspects, but also the social, economic, and political aspects, which are essential if you're going to change the culture and create a new market.

TAKEAWAYS

- You must remember that challenging the status quo will be threatening to the establishment.

- If you're going to change the culture and create a new market, you need to understand social, economic, and political considerations as well as the technical aspects of your industry.

Managing Change

- You must be prepared for change. Disruptive technologies can mean that you have to learn new skills, change the players, or need new infrastructure.

ABOUT THE CONTRIBUTORS

John Abele is the cofounder of Boston Scientific, the worldwide developer, manufacturer, and marketer of medical devices.

Boston Scientific's history began in the late 1960s, when Mr. Abele acquired an equity interest in Medi-tech, Inc., a research and development company focused on developing alternatives to traditional surgery.

In 1979, Mr. Abele partnered with Pete Nicholas to buy Medi-tech, and together they formed Boston Scientific Corporation. Since its public offering in 1992, Boston Scientific has undergone an aggressive acquisition strategy, assembling the lines of business that allow it to continue to be a leader in the medical industry.

Peter Birch is the former chairman of Land Securities Group and the current senior independent director of Trinity Mirror.

Mr. Birch worked for Nestlé in the United Kingdom, Switzerland, Singapore, and Malaysia from 1958 to 1965. He held various positions between 1965 and 1984 with Gillette Industries, the consumer products group. This included time as

About the Contributors

managing director of Gillette UK Ltd. and group general manager for Africa, the Middle East, and Eastern Europe.

His next fourteen years were spent as chief executive of Abbey National, during which time he oversaw the successful transition of the building society into a bank.

Peter Birch is the former chairman of Land Securities, the provider of commercial accommodation and property services, and also of Kensington Group, the financial services organization. He stepped down in December 2006.

David Brandon is the chairman and CEO of Domino's Pizza.

Mr. Brandon started his career at Procter & Gamble, where he worked in sales management. In 1979, following his tenure at Procter & Gamble, he moved to Valassis Communications, Inc., a company in the sales promotion and coupon industries. He became president and chief executive officer in 1989, a position he held until 1998, while additionally taking on the role of chairman in the last two years.

Brandon subsequently moved to Domino's Pizza, and has been the company's chairman and chief executive officer since March 1999.

William Harrison retired as chairman, director, and CEO of JPMorgan Chase & Co. in December 2006. Mr. Harrison held this title since November 2001.

About the Contributors

From January 2001 until that time he held the position of president and CEO. Prior to the merger with J.P. Morgan & Co., Incorporated, Mr. Harrison had been chairman and CEO of the Chase Manhattan Corporation, a position he assumed in January 2000.

He had held the same responsibilities at the Chemical Bank prior to its merger with Chase in 1996. In 1978 he moved to London to take responsibility for the bank's U.K. business, and in 1982 was promoted to division head of Europe. Mr. Harrison returned to the United States in 1983 to run the U.S. corporate division, and was put in charge of the bank's global Banking and Corporate Finance group three years later.

Mr. Harrison is currently vice chairman of Chemical Bank and a director for Merck & Co.

Mel Lagomasino is the CEO at Asset Management Advisors, a multifamily office that provides independent advice to families of substantial wealth. Asset Management Advisors is an affiliate of SunTrust Banks, Inc.

Prior to joining AMA in November 2005, she was chairman and CEO of JPMorgan Private Bank, one of the largest providers of wealth management services worldwide, with more than $300 billion in client assets and over $1.5 billion in revenues.

Ms. Lagomasino's career with JPMorgan Chase began when she joined The Chase Manhattan International Private Bank in 1983 as Vice President and Team Leader for Latin America. In 1989 she

About the Contributors

was named head of the Private Bank Western Hemisphere Area. She became the global private bank executive in 1997, in charge of Chase's worldwide private banking business. Before joining Chase she was a vice president at Citibank, and prior to that worked at the United Nations.

Ms. Lagomasino is a current director of Avon Products, Inc., and a former director of Coca-Cola.

Shelly Lazarus is the chairman and CEO of Ogilvy & Mather Worldwide.

Ms. Lazarus has since been with the agency network for more than three decades. After rising through the ranks of account management and playing a pivotal role on many of Ogilvy & Mather's signature accounts—including American Express, Kraft, and Unilever—she left the general agency to become the general manager for Ogilvy & Mather Direct in the United States.

Her success there led to positions of increasing responsibility, from president of Ogilvy & Mather Advertising in New York in 1991, to president of Ogilvy North America three years later. Just one year later, she became chief operating officer and president of Ogilvy & Mather Worldwide. She was named CEO in 1996 and became chairman in 1997.

Maurice Lévy is the chairman and CEO of Publicis Groupe.

Mr. Lévy joined Publicis, one of the world's largest advertising and media services conglomer-

About the Contributors

ates, in 1971. He was given responsibility for its data processing and information technology systems.

However, he moved swiftly up the organization, being appointed corporate secretary in 1973, managing director in 1976, and chair and CEO of Publicis Conseil in 1981.

He then became vice chair of Publicis Groupe in 1986 and vice chair of the management board in 1988.

John Roberts is a recently retired CEO of United Utilities.

Mr. Roberts graduated from Liverpool University and joined Manweb. After working his way up the company he became finance director in 1984, then managing director in 1991. He was appointed chief executive a year later.

He then became CEO of South Wales Electricity, being at the helm during its acquisition by Hyder, and was then appointed CEO of Hyder Utilities. He was appointed CEO of United Utilities in September 1999 and retired from the company in March 2006.

Sir Nick Scheele is currently the chancellor at the University of Warwick, a position he accepted in October 2001.

A thirty-eight-year veteran of Ford Motor Company, he retired from Ford in 2005 as president and member of the board of directors. In 1992, he became vice chairman of Jaguar Cars, quickly rising

About the Contributors

to become chairman and CEO. In July 2000, he became president of Ford Europe, and is credited with having directed the increasingly successful transformation of Ford's European business. In October 2001, he was appointed president and COO of Ford's global operations as well as a member of its board of directors.

Paul Skinner is the chairman of Rio Tinto, the global mining and minerals company dual-listed in the United Kingdom and Australia.

Mr. Skinner has spent his career working in the extractive industry. He spent forty years with the Royal Dutch/Shell group of companies, joining the group as a student in 1963. During his career there he worked in all of Shell's main businesses, including senior appointments in the United Kingdom, Greece, Nigeria, New Zealand, and Norway.

From 1999 he was CEO of the Group's global oil products business, and was managing director of The Shell Transport and Trading Company (and a group managing director) from 2000 to 2003. Mr. Skinner joined the board of Rio Tinto as a nonexecutive director in 2001 and became chairman in 2003.

James Strachan is the former chairman of the Audit Commission, the public services regulator and watchdog—a position he held from 2002 until January 2006.

About the Contributors

Mr. Strachan read economics and English at Cambridge University and subsequently worked in London for fourteen years as both a commercial banker and investment banker. This culminated in his becoming managing director of Merrill Lynch in London, and a board member of Merrill Lynch International.

Strachan moved into the voluntary and public sectors in 1994 and became CEO of the RNID (Royal National Institute for Deaf People), a role he held from 1997 until 2002. He is now its chairman.

Stephen Tindale is the current executive director of Greenpeace UK.

Mr. Tindale started his career as a diplomat. His four years in the Foreign Office included a year at the British Embassy in Pakistan. After that he joined Friends of the Earth, where he was the organization's air pollution campaigner.

Following this, he spent two years at the Fabian Society. He then went to work for Chris Smith MP, the recently appointed Shadow Environment Secretary. After two years in this role he moved to the Institute for Public Policy Research (IPPR), where he worked on green taxes and energy policy.

Mr. Tindale then became the director of Green Alliance. However he was taken from this position after the 1997 elections to be special adviser to Michael Meacher when he became Environment Minister. Mr. Tindale held this position for two

About the Contributors

years before deciding he would be more effective trying to influence change from outside the system, and moved subsequently to Greenpeace UK.

Laura Tyson is a professor and former dean at the Haas School of Business at the University of California, Berkeley.

Professor Tyson was previously the dean of the London Business School and former White House National Economic Adviser. Professor Tyson joined as the School's dean in 2002 and left that position at the end of 2006. Before that, she had been dean at the Haas School of Business and Professor of Economics and Business Administration at the University of California.

Professor Tyson served in the Clinton administration from January 1993 to December 1996. Between February 1995 and December 1996 she served as the president's National Economic Adviser and was the highest-ranking woman in the Clinton White House. Prior to this appointment she served as the sixteenth chairman of the White House Council of Economic Advisers, the first woman to hold that post.

Currently, Professor Tyson also serves as director for Morgan Stanley, Eastman Kodak Company, and AT&T (formerly Ameritech Corp).

John Whybrow is currently the chairman of Wolseley, the world's leading distributor of heating and

About the Contributors

plumbing products for the professional market. He first joined Wolseley in 1997 as a director.

Mr. Whybrow's career started at the English Electric Company in 1968. He originally joined Philips in 1970, rising to become managing director of the Philips Power Semiconductors and Microwave business in 1987.

In 1993 he was appointed chairman and managing director of Philips Electronics UK. He was then made president and CEO of Philips Lighting Holding in the Netherlands.

From May 1998 until April 2002 he held the post of executive vice president of Royal Philips Electronics, where he also took board responsibility for leading quality and e-business initiatives within the company.

Mr. Whybrow is also the director of the consumer electronics retailer Dixons.

ACKNOWLEDGMENTS

First and foremost, a heartfelt thanks goes to all of the executives who have shared their hard-earned experience and battle-tested insights for the Lessons Learned series.

Angelia Herrin, at Harvard Business School Publishing, consistently offered unwavering support, good humor, and counsel from the inception of this ambitious project.

Julia Ely, Hollis Heimbouch, and David Goehring provided invaluable editorial direction, perspective, and encouragement. Much appreciation goes to Jennifer Lynn for her research and diligent attention to detail. Many thanks to the entire HBSP team of designers, copy editors, and marketing professionals who helped bring this series to life.

Finally, thanks to our fellow cofounder James MacKinnon and the entire Fifty

Acknowledgments

Lessons team for the tremendous amount of time, effort, and steadfast support they devoted to this project.

—Adam Sodowick
  Andy Hasoon
  Directors and Cofounders
  Fifty Lessons

EXCLUSIVE READER OFFER

You've Read Them, Now
WATCH THEM

Visit www.fiftylessons.com/hbsp and watch free, bonus videos from the world's top business leaders.

These videos are exclusive to you at no extra charge.

There's no need to register, simply enter **code 2020** to get instant access to the wisdom and experience of the world's most talented leaders.

www.fiftylessons.com/hbsp

HARVARD BUSINESS SCHOOL PRESS